Nora Maccoby

Identity Cartography: Maps and Symbols for the Heterarchy

OCTOBER 2018   WASHINGTON DC

Nobody Owns You:
A Survival Map for Liberty
OIL ON CANVAS 30" X 24"

COVER:

The Day the Runners came
from Standing Rock
OIL ON CANVAS 20" X 16"

So How Do We Build A Democratic Heterarchy?

We start with our own selves:

To power our center, become balanced, and integrate with others in peace and common purpose for the welfare of the whole.

Build bridges over chaos. Unify and serve justice with mercy.

The following is from Black Elk Speaks: Being the life story of a holy man of the Ogallala Sioux (1961), as told to John Neihardt

"The first peace, which is the most important, is that which comes within the souls of people when they realize their relationship, their oneness, with the universe and all its powers, and when they realize that at the center of the universe dwells Wakan-Tanka, and that this center is really everywhere, it is within each of us. This is the real peace, and the others are but reflections of this. The second peace is that which is made between two individuals, and the third is that which is made between two nations. But above all you should understand that there can never be peace between nations until there is known that true peace, which, as I have often said, is within the souls of men." A good nation I will make live.

"Our tepees were round like the nests of birds, and these were always set in a circle, the nation's hoop."

"The sacred hoop of my people was one of many hoops that made one circle, wide as daylight and as starlight, and in the center grew one mighty flowering tree to shelter all the children of one mother and one father. And I saw that it was holy.

Building Bridges is a High
OIL ON CANVAS 20" X 16"

Crazy Horse dreamed and went into the world where there is nothing but the spirits of all things. That is the real world that is behind this one, and everything we see here is something like a shadow from that one.

The power of the world always works in circles, and everything tries to be round. In the old days when we were a strong and happy people, all our power came to us from the sacred hoop of the nation, and so long as the hoop was unbroken the people flourished.

Everything the Power of the World does is done in a circle. The sky is round, and I have heard that the earth is round like a ball, and so are all the stars. The wind, in its greatest power whirls. Birds make their nest in circles, for theirs is the same religion as ours. The sun comes forth and goes down again in a circle. The moon does the same and both are round. Even the seasons form a great circle in their changing, and always come back again to where they were. **The life of a man is a circle from childhood to childhood, and so it is in everything where power moves. Our tepees were round like the nests of birds, and these were always set in a circle, the nation's hoop.**

A Map for Building Happiness
OIL ON CANVAS 30" X 24"

"My work is focused on finding the point between form and formlessness, and the notion of light as an active intelligence within universal codes found in nature on Earth, and in space itself. As we find ourselves in chaotic cultural upheaval, my interest has been in re-casting Hesiod's Catalogue of Women — also known as the Ehoiai ('Ηοῖαι, Ancient: [e:hói.ai]) — into a new modality, a progressive paradigm where women support each other and find the rebalancing of justice through their own evolution as sentient beings to build common ground for a healthy, vibrant, prosperous world. The journey of the work is then a navigation of space/time, through new symbols. A cartography for power, based not on patriarchy or matriarchy, but a heterarchy; to power the center and dance with friends." —Nora Maccoby

Identity Cartography
OIL ON CANVAS 24" X 58"

Identity Cartography: Maps and Symbols for the Heterarchy

What is Identity? Is it the definition of our material form, a craft of genetics, color and sex? Or can we be judged, as Martin Luther King Jr. offered, by the "content of our character"? Are we to be defined as tribal demographics, ghettoized and profiled by social media artificial intelligence and predatory special interests abusing a free society and destroying the very means of survival, of clean air, water and soil in the process? Or can we as citizens awaken to our potential and craft a sustainable, just and prosperous society?

Guardian of Bridges, Avenger of Walls
OIL ON CANVAS 24" X 58"

What does success in postmodernity mean when the accumulation of wealth is made at the expense of survival of the whole? Are your Nestle investments worth the pillaging and destruction of basic rights to water? When The Founding Fathers (and Mothers and Slaves) established America, they copied the democratic system of the Iroquois Nation, but left out the final process of decision-making that had to consider the welfare of the seven generations that would have to deal with the consequences. This final circle was The Circle of Grandmothers.

A status quo that cares only for immediate gratification and holds greed as a proper value will end in all our destruction. The pathetic truth is that we live in degrees of denial, glorifying a passive consumer culture of throwaway disposable things. We have technology that can turn our trash to fuel, provide sustainability for the poor, but greed and business as usual have no time for common sense. We dump these poisons into piles, to seep into our soil and water. The majority of the world literally lives in our trash.

Building the Sacred Hoop:
A path to peace
OIL ON CANVAS 30" X 30"

The Greek ideals of "democracy" came out of a society where only men were free and women were objects or slaves. In Hesiod's Catalogue of Women, we find goddess archetypes sabotaging each other, perpetuating their own weaknesses. In the re-casting of them, I have discovered that when women support each other, they birth a foundation, an order against the perpetual onslaught of chaos that is part of our existence on this miraculous planet, traveling through the great galaxy and universe.

We live in a time of chaotic social and environmental change. But so it is also true that in great transition lays tremendous opportunity. If we are to seize this moment, we may see the inheritance that we hold now in the foundations that support our democracy. We must define success for ourselves, for the value of our time on Earth, find a way to support the common good, and make it possible for the generations that follow us to also have a chance at life. We stand at the crossroad of great choice - universal existence or extinction.

I am the sum of both immigrants and soldiers in the Revolutionary war. My parents gave birth to me while working in Mexico with Erich Fromm and Ivan Illich, who had escaped the Nazis, other social theorists like Margaret Mead and DT Suzuki, and were working to find ways to develop a biophilic, life-loving world that also incorporated the basic rights and truths of indigenous peoples.

My mother, Sandylee, her grandmother, Adeline Perry, aunt, Doris Walker Pritchard (also an early founder of Friends of the Earth) and my sister Izette Folger, (co-founder of Transformer), were and are great painters and colorists. My mother believed that God was color itself and watching her spend hours in meditative concentration while painting portraits of her subjects (my 3 siblings, numerous dogs, patrons, included) discovering the integration of the minutia of faces and bodies with spirit and soul was eternally fascinating. I was not interested in painting until 1994, and primarily drew, made super 8 films, and composed music. I began violin at age 5 with Sheila Johnson, who at that time was merging eastern Suzuki method with western classical, folk, pop, and performing in a children's orchestra in Jordan and England, and at home for the sick children in the DC children's hospital. It was an incredible education of the power of music to heal and activate change in different worlds and cultures. My first internship was in high school writing dialogue for Video Soul, one of the first television shows on BET, the network that she and her husband were creating. Sheila taught me more than music, she showed me the impossible was possible if you focused, persevered and persisted against all odds of ridicule, doubt and fear.

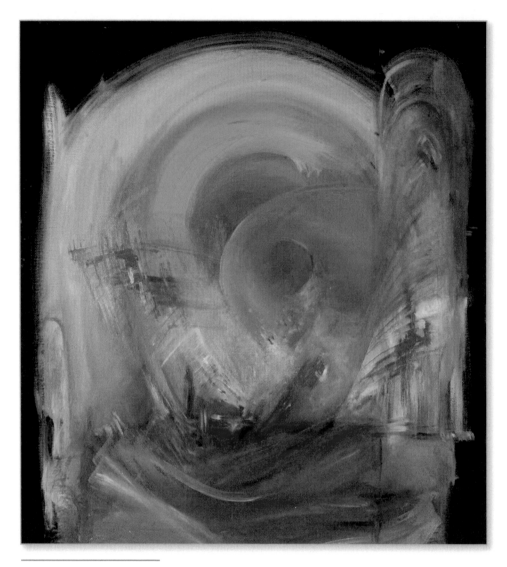

Time Walkers 2
OIL ON CANVAS 20" X 16"

I attended both public and Quaker school at Sidwell Friends, studied theater and government at Oberlin College, and got an MFA in film directing at The American Film Institute. I studied Color Healing at the Center of New Directions, founded as The College of Psychotherapeutics by Ronald P. Beesley, a painter who had fought with the Resistance against the Nazis during WW2. It was here I discovered the power and values of color, light, and paint, including studying Tibetan Buddhist mandalas and mantras, looking for formulas and tools with which to craft new understandings of ancient wisdom.

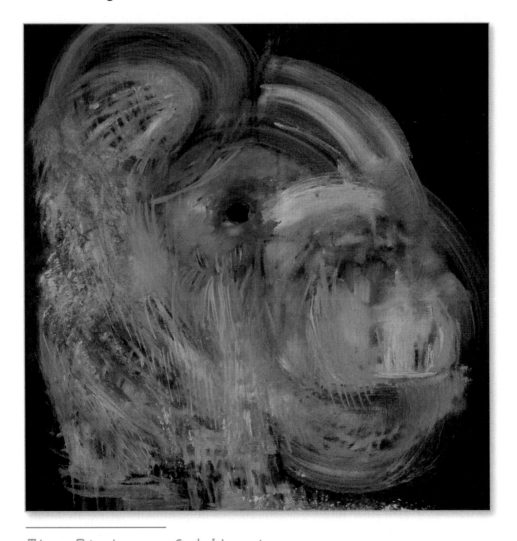

The Stakes of Liberty,
Stand Strong in Chaos
OIL ON CANVAS 20" X 16"

As a filmmaker, I saw firsthand the power and unleashing of the Pandora's box of dreams, visions, and nightmares on the masses, both good and bad, all imprinting on the collective consciousness and inevitably, the AI. What were we tapping into and unleashing? After a decade in the entertainment industry, the politicization of our film, Buffalo Soldiers, the aftermath of 9-11, and a near death experience, I felt reality was more important than fantasy, so I returned to DC to serve my country by building bridges for the common purpose of basic rights like clean air, water, soil, and industries of peace.

Returning to the National Capitol Region as an adult, I wanted to restore the values of the original (post-diluvian) indigenous Americans from whom we had crafted many of our concepts of democracy, the Native Americans. I felt that in the moral bankruptcy of the 1% consuming the majority of the world's resources while using perpetual war to drive suffering for profit, we had little time to bicker and degenerate into weaker identity profiling that was turning into a Maoist reversal of the dominant paradigm. I was more interested in Evolution than Revolution.

Moving forward, I found partners on all sides of politics and party who were also eager to create a third column based on common sense, mutual survival, and a mechanism to invest in our own people, rather than at their expense and ultimate destruction.

Black Elk's words echoed in my head. The great leader of the Lakota Sioux had said the spirit of the Land will speak through all the people on it, no matter their color, creed or sex, it matters not. We are the land and the air and the soil, for we are made of Earth and stardust.

I had a vision that one day the Lakota would come to Washington and build a circle in front of the White House. I dreamt that we would build a third, center column to wage peace between left and right. We would agree to partner with nature, instead of raping it, and kick-start new industries developed by the innovations coming out of our own tax-funded laboratories.

The options of Free Will in a
Limitless Universe
OIL ON CANVAS 20" X 16"

It was the most unlikely allies of soldiers tired of fighting as mercenary forces for oil companies and the business interests of warfare, that we built a movement that was based on protecting the foundation of life itself: America's blood and treasure. The movement was based on simple truths: clean air, water and soil is national security, sanity, and our base principles of value.

This movement became centralized in The Energy Conversation, and thanks to activators like Mitzi Wertheim, a grandmother and first highest ranking woman in the Navy, and grandfathers like Lt Col Bill Holmberg, and so many others, ultimately became a collaboration of 29 government agencies and departments working together to "listen, learn, share, connect, collaborate" to transition to a clean energy future powered by peace, not war. Peace is profitable.

The Energy Conversation lasted almost 5 years, with a network of 8,000+ citizens in and out of government working towards a common goal. I served as Senior Communications Specialist for The Energy Conversation, and on the Power Surety Task Force, for the Office of the Secretary of Defense, before political interests destroyed this effort at open dialogue and contextual understanding of energy as the foundation of our republic.

With my husband, Todd Hathaway, an Army Nuclear and Counterproliferation Officer, we continued to actively support all energy efforts that could neutralize our dependence on suicidal energy needs. We formed PSCI, the Potomac Sustainable Communities Initiative, created The Green and Blue Salon, to bring truth to power, with artist Mara Haseltine, her father William Haseltine, Richard Marks, and collaborators including the Swedish government, Chinese environmental movement, and the growing sharing based communities, developing innovative technologies, networks and processes for a common future on Earth. This led to intersectional work with DARPA, The Defense Advanced Research Agency, in the area of The Study of the Weaponization-Warfare of Social Media, Combatting the Trafficking of Humans and Animals to Fund Terrorism, and Virtual Reality.

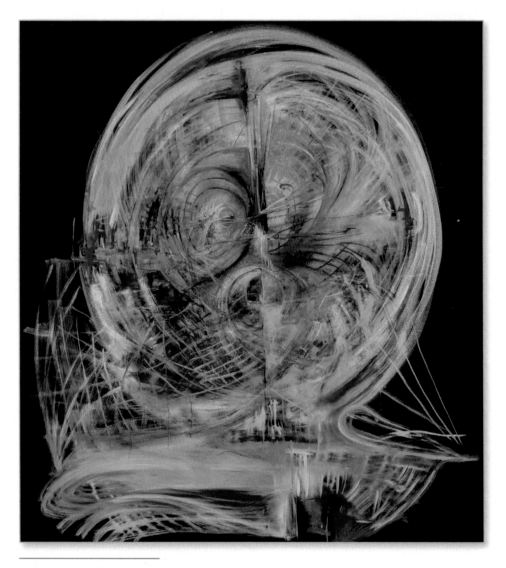

Black Elk speaks
OIL ON CANVAS 5" X 5"

I began collaborating with innovators like NOIRFLUX, doing interactive 3D immersive experience with my paintings, turning them into interdimensional light sculptures. This intersected with gravitational physics and holographic sound and healing work. I used the paintings as architecture for space and time travel studies and learned from NOIRFLUX's 30 years study to understand human interaction with Light and Color itself.

Eagle rises in the high blue surf
OIL ON CANVAS 30" X 20"

Working in a new art form was inspiring, yet America was under serious threat and not enough people understood what was happening. DARPA's Social Media study was de-funded exactly as the growing psychological warfare using identity politics, psychosis-triggering programming, and outrageous libel on Americans, as well as other targets, was being ramped up to create mass confusion, distrust of civil authority, and civil war. It was now easier to manipulate a mob through fake news than to build a conventional army. Unable to awaken others from their comfort bubbles of denial and normalcy to this threat, two friends from DARPA, Paul "PK" Kozemchak and Michael Hsui, and I, developed a television show called Deepstate about the battle at the end of time and Ezekiel's choice of paths; between good DARPA and bad DARPA, the negative threat or the positive potentials of artificial intelligence; the challenges of state sponsored malicious actors against open networks in a free society and the gullibility of a critically thinking challenged population drenched in perpetual onslaught of "entertainment" while basic rights to clean air, water and soil were being stolen from the people in front of our eyes.

In August 2016, under threat from oil companies eager to exploit the land, and against the logic and common sense that this would destroy the water supply for millions of people, the young people from Standing Rock, Lakota Sioux Nation, decided to take matters into their own hands.

Tribe of Many Colors
OIL ON CANVAS 30" X 30"

The runners from Standing Rock, North Dakota were between the ages of 12 and 24. The vision became real. We met them in front of the White House and together with the smallest children to the tallest young person, the first circle was built, to state the truth and make a stand for their survival and our survival and all our children to come: Water is Life.

This simple truth was very challenging for the greedy and the blind who worship money over life itself. And what followed in the next weeks and months was both a massing of good and evil. Of the attack on the American people by hostile forces, both state and corporate sponsored, wishing to divide and conquer Americans by asymmetric methods, to turn brother against sister, and cloud the truth from all eyes. The weaponization of the internet and the fantasy of 24 hour trance-inducing entertaining news washed the Republic into disarray and chaos. Words were no longer possible. Walls and chasms erupted where bridges need to hold.

Exactly one year later, while making homage to the sacred waters of the North East of America, I asked for direct guidance, and received a simple yet profound message, akin to a mandala: Power the Center and Dance with Your Friends.

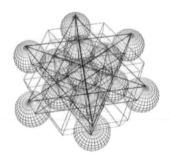

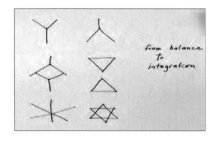
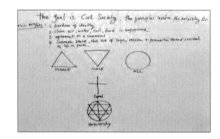

When I was a child, my father, would show me the story of the Star of David, also written inside the pyramids of Egypt. The future of humankind is written here, he said, for it is the story from balance to integration of the male and female principles. It will not be a matriarchy or a patriarchy but a heterarchy.

To Build a Heterarchy: Map and Instructions
To be viewed in all directions   OIL ON CANVAS 24" X 58"

(And when this symbol is made 3D it becomes a "merkaba", the mystical vehicle of transmutation and transcendence from this material plane of existence.)

Researching the modern concepts of "heterarchy", I came across the work of neurophysiologist and cybernetician, Warren Sturgis McCulloch, who in 1945, refreshed interest in an organizational principle which would become fundamental to modern computers and artificial intelligence.

No matter how many hierarchies there may be, the processing of information and the growth of intelligence is most effectively powered by systems of heterarchy.

Sisters and Brothers of Democracy
OIL ON CANVAS 36" X 60"

Time Machine
OIL ON CANVAS 24" X 30"

What is Leadership in a Heterarchy?

"In a heterarchy, leadership shifts according to which person has the skills needed at the time. In Native American tribes, one person might lead a hunting party, another a war party, another a spiritual celebration. The group determines who will lead the heterarchy and the leader only remains leader as long as the group determines it.

Now in the most advanced tech organization, heterarchy returns, because different competencies are needed to design, program, and market products. But heterarchy does not just depend on fitting the right person to the role. It also requires habits of the heart that create trusting collaboration.

The most effective organizations are democratic heterarchies. Everyone shares the same purpose and values and people choose the leaders they need and they remain leaders only as long as the people need them."

—Michael Maccoby, (On Leadership in a Heterarchy, 2018)

Map for surfing through the chaos
of dissonance
OIL ON CANVAS 30" X 24"

Power the Center and Dance with Your Friends
OIL ON CANVAS 36" X 60"

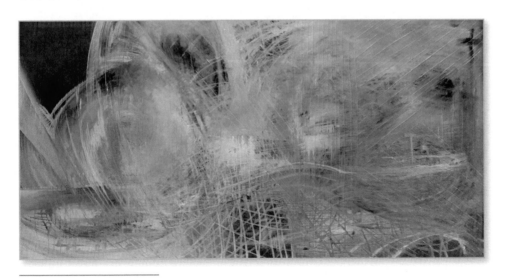

The Delight: To Activate Free Will
OIL ON CANVAS 30" X 24"

In the Field of Becoming Us
OIL ON CANVAS 30" X 60"

Nora Maccoby

Identity Cartography: Maps and Symbols for the Heterarchy

The Woman's National Demorcratic Club
1526 New Hampshire Ave NW, Wash DC 20036

Oil paintings on view
Sept 6 - Nov 27

Graphic Design by Grazia Montalto

Published by ART4US
Back cover photo by Ariane Moody

NORA MACCOBY

is a conceptual and multimedia artist working at the nexus of science, technology, and political philosophy. Her drawings and oil paintings are the architectural groundwork for her collaboration in 3D interactive video art with the NOIRFLUX collective. She is also a screenwriter, Bongwater (1998), Buffalo Soldiers (2003), and the author of The Energy Conversation: the first 3 years (CNA, 2009). Her novel, The Intelligence, will be available this fall (RMP, 2018).

Made in the USA
Middletown, DE
29 November 2018